# Deadly Deception
# in the Church

# Deadly Deception in the Church

Tyrone Everett

| Library of Congress Control Number: | | 2009904045 |
| --- | --- | --- |
| ISBN: | Hardcover | 978-1-4415-3166-7 |
| | Softcover | 978-1-4415-3165-0 |

This book was printed in the United States of America.

**To order additional copies of this book, contact:**
Xlibris Corporation
1-888-795-4274
www.Xlibris.com
Orders@Xlibris.com
60839

# Contents

# Dedication

To my wife Rhonda, and sons: Shaun and his wife Shantae, Jason, and Joseph.

To my granddaughter Ariana and sister Love Powell and my niece Iyana.

For my mother Jean Powell and late brother Michael.

Also to the friends who encouraged me to write the books: Carlton and Chris Carter who helped me tremendously.

Finally to you, the reader, may you understand what the Spirit is saying.

# Church In Prophecy

What time is it? How many of you would like to know where the church is in biblical prophecy? The key to discerning when a prophecy is fulfilled is to know its time of visitation. In Luke 12:54-56, Christ says to the Pharisees (religious leaders of that time) that they could discern the weather, but they could not discern the signs of the times that were upon them. The leaders could not discern that Jesus was the Messiah, fulfilling the prophecies spoken of Him by the prophets. Let's look at a few prophesies concerning Jesus as the Messiah. In the book of Isaiah 7:10-16, we find that Christ would be born of a virgin; also in chapter 53, Isaiah speaks of Christ's mission; and in chapter 6, it talks about the religious leaders.

The Pharisees knew what was written concerning the messiah but could not correlate the prophecies within their own time. Another example of this problem is shown when people read prophetic scriptures as in the book of Acts 8:26-40. The Ethiopian asked Philip, "Is this prophecy speaking of someone from the past or of someone in the future?" Then of course, Philip explained to him how the scriptures were speaking of Jesus. There are many scriptures that Jesus fulfilled in His life span, and I included some of them in the back of this book for you to study.

The problem we have in interpreting the scriptures is very similar to problems these men had during their time—understanding when prophecies are being fulfilled. Even our religious leaders have the same attitudes as the Pharisees and cannot see it. We find that there are some religious organizations that have predicted the return of Christ or the second coming; not only were they wrong, but believers would continue to follow them!

During the return of the Jews to Jerusalem back in the 1940's, some evangelicals were telling their followers that it was the end of the world and God was about to pour out His wrath upon the world because of their sins. People were selling their homes, making under ground bunkers, and preparing the best way they could afford. Of course, nothing happened as taught by these religious leaders because they made the same mistake the Pharisees made in their day. That mistake was, taking a series of prophecies found in the scriptures and applying them to current events that they do not apply to. In a way its like if you could, put all the prophecies in a blender and pushing the frappé button.

The Jews understood that the Messiah had to fulfill all the prophecies concerning Him and make Jerusalem the center of world worship. These leaders did not understand how to correctly categorize the prophecies for different times and events. During the year 1998, some computer software designers said computers would have problems when the year 2000 would appear and could cause computers to shut down or malfunction. Well, religious leaders were telling their congregations that the rise of the anti-Christ was at hand and that the mark of the beast was about to unfold. Again, people started buying all these generators and food, some sold their homes and prepared for what they thought would be THE LAST DAYS.

I felt this way too until, while preparing a message, the Spirit of God revealed something to me that I did not consider. The times that God prepared would not be based on man's inventions. The times of fulfilling prophecies will be set by God's events such as the great earthquake as mentioned in Revelation 6:12-17. **Now technology may be used as a tool but not as a sign of fulfillment of prophecy**.

Even today, men are making this error, using technology as a sign of Bible prophecy such as the bar code or the RFID chip that can be planted under your skin, equating this with the mark of the beast. So which is it, the bar code or the RFID chip? The Bible does not make it clear how Satan will set up a system concerning how one can buy or sell food—whether you have a mark on your forehead or your right hand. Instead of using technology, has anyone ever considered using the Church! Surprised? Yes, the Bride of Christ and the rejection of Christ teachings, as taught by modern theological seminaries.

They have caused a division in believers based on the following teaching: "THE RAPTURE," and other teachings of significant character. Some men have spent a lot of energy trying to figure out what only the GodHead knows. To me, the interpretation of the rapture is like a big wrench thrown in the gears of prophetic study to have the believer concentrate more on when Christ is coming than what is actually being fulfilled now. In 1 Thessalonians 4:13-18, and 5:1-9 and in 1 Corinthians 15:51-58 and Philippians 3:21 (read before moving on to familiarize yourself with these specific scriptures about the rapture), the rapture is prophesied. So from these particular scriptures and the book of Revelation and Matthew chapter 24, we have three distinct times when men have taught about the return of Christ. The teaching of pre-tribulation, middle, and post-tribulation.

Two of these positions can cause the following example: Read Luke 12:45, notice what the servants said, "The Lord delays His coming." Now what could have caused this man to say "the Lord delays His coming"? Unless he was expecting a specific time he felt the Lord should have returned. If I told you I would check with you later, you might think I will call you or come by and see you later, right? But if I did neither, you might call the next day and say, "I thought you were going to get back with me yesterday." Because of what I said, I made you *expect* me to do what I said that day.

**Expectancy** can cause disappointment such as the case when the people found out that Christ was not going to return as predicted by their Church leaders; some followers even turned away from their faith! Ever read the story of the "Boy Who Cried Wolf"? He was a shepherd who was supposed to scream "wolf" whenever a wolf would appear, and the townspeople would come out to help protect the sheep. Well, one day the boy got bored and screamed "wolf" and the townspeople came out only to find him asleep and no wolf. So the boy waited awhile and did it again, and the townspeople came out just as before; this happened two more times. So one day the shepherd boy saw a wolf coming for real and screamed, "WOLF, WOLF!" and no one came to help him and the wolf destroyed many sheep. So today, when I testify to people about prophetic things, they say, "People have been saying that for years!" I believe Satan, the enemy, is behind this tactic, so that when he really comes, no one will take heed as it is written in Revelations 13, "He shall make war with the saints and overcome them."

So the best way to be prepared is, to know the Word and seek understanding from the Holy Spirit. Prophecy is used to warn the children of God like a weather station is used to warn towns of approaching hazardous storms. Just as you would take precautions to protect your life and possessions, protect yourself from the events that the scriptures warn shall come upon the world.

# Chapter 1

## CURRENT PROPHECIES

What are some of the hidden prophecies today? Just like the Jews of old, we would have a hard time understanding the Old Testament prophecies or overlook them just like the Ethiopian in the book of Acts. Try reading the Old Testament and find everything that was prophetic. You will see why the Jewish reader had a hard time understanding everything that was prophesied about the Messiah. So let's look at a prophecy that is overlooked, what I call Prophetic Burps because they seem out of place with the text.

For instance in Isaiah 7 the Lord asked King Ahaz for a sign; and then the Lord said, "I will give you a sign 'Behold a virgin shall conceive.'" Well, if you read the text, you have to ask yourself, "what does a woman conceiving a baby have anything to do with the current situation at hand?" Now imagine these types of prophetic burps all over the Old Testament and yes, in the New Testament as well. Read Luke 23:29 *"For, behold, the days are coming in which they shall say, Blessed are the barren, and the wombs that never bare, and the paps which never gave suck."* Now you may have never heard women talking about having babies, but I have heard many women say to other women who cannot have children, "Girl, you don't know how lucky you are not to be able to have any children, I wish I didn't have any." Or, "You don't need any birth control that messes up your body, that's why I gained all this weight."

Now in Jesus's time, it was just the opposite. If you could not have a child, you were considered cursed by God! This is a major difference of our time compared to Jesus time over two thousand years ago. In conjunction with children, we also find Jesus talking about another scene, same time frame. In Matthew 18:3-7, we see Jesus talking about adults abusing children, *"But who so shall offend one of these little ones which believe in me, it were better for him that a millstone were hanged about his neck, and that he were drowned in the depth of the sea."* In the next verse, Jesus says this offense must take place! (This prophecy will see its totality when Satan sets up his system in the future, when a woman can only buy food for her baby if she accepts the mark). You see how these prophetic burps come and are ignored; they are simply overlooked for whatever reason.

It is sad that a lot of these offenses take place in the church! The biggest abuse is sexual, I have talked to so many men who turned gay because a relative, who was a deacon or the pastor himself or a priest molested them and then these preachers have the audacity to speak against homosexuals while they are committing the same act! No wonder so many gay people stay out of the church! The church's biggest problem is not homosexuals, the church's biggest problem is sexual immorality! How many gay people do you know are in the majority of evangelical churches here in the South? Now we are starting to see a big move of gay right activists who are trying to prove the Bible accepts their lifestyle; maybe it's just a way to get back at the church for the pain they caused them.

But sin is sin. Are homosexuals' sins greater than adultery or a divorce that is not accepted under biblical conditions? As Paul says, "Neither will enter into the Kingdom of God." Preachers know that if they press the issue with sexual immorality in the church, they will lose members just as some Caucasian ministers know if they preached on racism in their church too much, they would lose members also. But they both agree on abortion and homosexuals, right? And they will preach hard on those subjects. As long as we keep the preaching on someone else, we gain more members. I say this to emphasize that sexual sins and racism are greater problems in the church than homosexuals and women having babies aborted.

Another prophetic burp is found in 2 Timothy 4:3-4, *"The time will come when they will not endure sound doctrine."* I have been telling people about the gospel for twenty-eight years, and I have seen some interesting changes. For instance back in the 1980s, I could speak with someone about God for a few minutes, and we were saying the sinner's prayer. In the '90s, it started taking a few weeks to a few months and now in 2000, I tried to share the

Gospel at my job for years, and no one converted! This is a result of other prophecies such as Daniel who wrote that "knowledge shall increase," and in Timothy it is written, "they will be forever learning and never able to come to the knowledge of the truth."

So what is it that they have learned? Everything! With the use of technology and the Internet, people can learn just about anything that is known to man. So everyone is a "subject matter expert." These intellectual individuals even tried to quote scripture to me and tell me what it meant! But when I asked them if they have ever read the Bible, they answered "no". Here is what they do: they "Cut and Paste" the text just like you can do on Microsoft Word. *Cut* and *Paste* are the terms I use to describe terms in the Bible taken out of context and put in another format to which it does not belong. For instance, they say, "The Bible says thou shalt not kill." So they would ask me, "Why were you in the military?" But the Bible was speaking about cold-blooded murder. When you read the Old Testament, you will find that God told the Israelites that when they go possess the land promised to them, they had to kill every man, woman (now hear this), and child! This is why some people think the Bible contradicts itself because they take the scriptures out of context, and insert them in the way they are not meant. You see how they "cut and paste" without having a full understanding about scriptures. Yet they feel they are experts on what the Bible means!

In 2 Timothy3:1-8, Paul is revealing things that pertain to our generation. *"This know also, that in the last days perilous times shall come. For men shall be lovers of their own selves, covetous, boasters, proud, blasphemers, disobedient to parents, unthankful, unholy. Without natural affection, trucebreakers, false accusers, incontinent, fierce, despisers of those that are good, traitors, heady, high minded, lovers of pleasures more than lovers of God."* People who are unsaved reason that this has been going on for years, but God had me to remind them how it was when I was a child growing up in Newport News, Virginia; how we could leave our house and go on vacation without locking our doors or windows, try that now! We could walk anywhere in the city without being molested, kidnapped, or murdered. Now these things were like this over forty plus years ago; that's not a long time, considering how things are now in this generation.

Morals have declined crazily because of selfishness, crime has increased 1,000 percent, children cannot be disciplined in school or homes, young men can't even fight with fist anymore, they have to use guns to settle their differences. Drugs are the biggest business in neighborhoods now. So many people are in debt because they cannot control their urge to buy. Waves of crimes such as road rage, church shootings and vandalism, robbing pizza drivers, or gang rape are increasing in numbers. There was even a wave of people cutting fetuses out of women! Churches are on almost every corner, yet crime is increasing.

Since the churches did not have some type of plan to witness to people on the streets, we may be too far behind to catch up. The fear of crime has caused so many of God's people to stay in the comforts of their homes after church. Now pastors have to start "street ministering" to address the problem and have had to start programs such as buying guns in an effort to save the community.

This could be the beginning of the saying, "Men's hearts are failing them because of fear." Fear for their life, that is, because of what they read in the papers or hear on the news. (For your information, about 97 percent of murders are from people who know each other, the other 3 percent are from stray bullets or a rare random acts of abduction and robbery including car theft.) So the news media reports on murders from around the country and the world, which gives the appearance of total chaos. It's not as bad as it is going to get, for these things are the beginning of sorrows. Now, one of the biggest prophecies Christ spoke of concerning the church is found in the parable about the sower of wicked seeds, which is found in Matthew 13:24-31. I will discuss this in further detail in Chapter 4.

# Chapter 2

## DANGER IN THE CHURCH

As we have seen in some of the scriptures in chapter 1, especially in Matthew chapter 24 and in 2 Timothy 3, wickedness increases, false preachers and teachers are bringing damnable teachings and revelations of God's Word. Knowledge shall increase especially through technology such as computers, Internet, TV, video, etc. *This knowledge shall cause confusion about the truth of God's Word;* men will begin to question and reason with the concepts of Christ's teachings. Because of crime and selfishness, the love of many Christians will grow cold, and love and devotion to God will decrease. This is Mark chapter 4 taking effect specifically the "heart of thorny ground." As Jesus taught in this parable, because of trials and tribulation for the world's sake, these Christians produced no fruit. As we can see, evil will increase, and most people in the church will say that, "It's because they took prayer out of school, and Jesus name out of public prayers." Man's intellect tells him it's because of the increase of population (although all these play a factor), but the real truth is that God's Word concerning current events are coming true.

I see some circles are bringing up Nostradamus, equating him to biblical prophecies as though by his own power, he could predict the future. Just as the Pharaoh's sorcerers in the time Moses produced some of the plagues that God performed, so the intellectuals believe it's nothing more than a tactic to have them follow some vain religion. This type of reasoning causes people not to endure the sound doctrine of scriptures as mentioned in 2 Timothy 3 and 4, "Now as Jannes and Jambres withstood Moses, so do these also resist the truth: men of corrupt minds, reprobate concerning the faith." This applies to cults in America such as Mormons and Jehovah's Witnesses. Ask any devout member of any religion whether they do believe their organization's teachings are biblically correct. They all will answer, "Absolutely or sure." For who believes their church leader will actually preach a boldface lie!? For this reason, "many shall be deceived, they in return will deceive others." I want you to understand something very important in your study of prophecies: "One prophetic event causes a behavior that leads us to another prophetic event." (As you have read from the previous paragraphs.) So now, let us look at some dangers concerning the church.

To start, we will look at what Christ spoke of as recorded by Matthew 24:4-5, "Take heed that no man deceives you.

For many shall come in My Name saying, 'I am Christ' and deceive many." The first thing we have to ask concerning this prophecy is, who is the "man" Jesus is referring to in this text? Who is that man who will try to deceive you? Is Jesus referring to a politician, a doctor, an auto mechanic, or a religious leader? You may say, all these men are! And I will have to agree, they all do. Jesus told His disciples, "Be careful of the leaven of the Pharisees and Sadducees." Meaning be careful of what they teach.

These men represent religious leaders! So let's reword what Jesus said, let's make it plain. **Do not allow religious leaders to deceive you!** Whose responsibility is it? That's right, it's **yours!** Jesus said, **"LET NO MAN DECEIVE YOU."** The other question you have to ask yourself is, "what are these religious leaders deceiving you with?" They are deceiving you with doctrine, teaching from their theological background, false interpretations of God's Word, false revelation of God's meaning (wrongly dividing the word; you know in mathematical division, if you mess up one step in the equation, your answer will end up wrong). Let us look at Revelation 2:12-17 for example, here we have the Church of Pergamos, and Jesus was telling them that some of their leaders were holding on to the "doctrine of the Nicolaitans," **which were the teachings He hated!** What doctrine they were, we do not have a clear understanding of, but I believe these doctrines are being practiced right under our nose. We could speculate as to what they are as men have tried, but there is not any concrete proof to back up anyone's claim. Of course, it would be nice to know what teaching Jesus was referring to, but we have enough "leaven" already to deal with today, and by accident, we may discover what doctrine Jesus hated (of course we could not know if we did or not).

It should be clear that "doctrine" is very important to the spiritual growth of all who truly have been "born again." Remember it is your responsibility to try those who call themselves leaders with the doctrine they teach you. That is, try them who call themselves "apostles, prophets, teachers, pastors, or whatever by the Spirit." That is, by the Spirit of Truth, who is the true author of what is truth concerning the scriptures. Let me say that again, **"Only the Holy Ghost is the Authority of ALL TRUTH!"** It is certainly not a religious institution; for what religion can claim they hold absolute truth with no error? Jesus says in the Gospel that the Holy Spirit shall reveal all truth to the believer concerning His relationship with Him even the deep mysteries not by men and their institutions. Although a religious institution may make such a claim, you should not follow them if you are a part of that religion. I have had threats made against me because I have tried these doctrines of men; threats like, "God is going to strike you dead because you tried God's anointed"; "Don't mess with God's anointed." They tried to make it seemed as though I am not God's anointed and that I should bow to them or something. Did not Jesus say we are all high priests unto the Lord? But these men breathe out threats like they are a prophet or something in the Old Testament when God did such things. Is the Holy Spirit in an Apostle greater than the Holy Spirit in a prophet? Or is the Holy Spirit the same in each person? So why would the Holy Spirit exalt Himself in one calling over the other? Read I Cor 12 to answer these questions.

When I was growing up in Newport News, Virginia, in the mid-'60s, churches used to proclaim, "If you are not a Catholic, Baptist, or Church of God, etc., you were in trouble for your salvation." It is not as evident now. I asked my nephew, while visiting him, "What religion has the monopoly on God?" In other words, what church, temple, synagogue, etc., has the absolute truth with no errors? I even use this when talking to people of different denominations to point out that only the Holy Spirit can reveal such truth. That is why, it is so important to walk in the Spirit and not with your intellect. Because I can take the scriptures and have them make sense intellectually and be spiritually wrong! This is why we have so many interpretations of the Bible now. Because if you read the Bible and five other people read the same passage of scripture, you will have six different opinions of what they mean. Now if we allow the Holy Spirit to give us all the interpretation, the Holy Spirit will not give me one understanding and give each other person something that contradicts everyone else, or else the Holy Spirit causes confusion and division. As we know from what Jesus taught, "A kingdom divided against itself cannot stand." So we know this is not of the Holy Spirit, for He will give us all the same understanding with no errors or contradictions. Most unbelievers always ask: "why are there so many different denominations" and now you have the answer.

The Bible teaches that Satan is the author of confusion. In 1 Corinthians 3:1-9, Paul is dealing with division in the church. What is the difference then if someone says, "I am Baptist," or if someone says, "I'm Pentecostal, or I'm Catholic"? Are we considered carnal according to Paul? We know it is not the Holy Spirit that is causing the division, so it has to be man. What do you mean, anyway, when you say, "I am Baptist or Pentecostal"? Are you saying, I have a set of beliefs that I'm comfortable with, or are you saying I believe that the doctrine of my religion is the most accurate? Is the church so proud that no one can humble themselves to be one church? I know these are some difficult questions, but they have to be asked, so we may start moving in the direction of the Holy Spirit.

# Chapter 3

## FALSE PROPHETS AND TEACHERS

The second dangerous work to look out for is many false prophets and teachers shall arise and deceive many (Matt. 24:11). As you can see, many Christians did not take heed because "many were deceived." So it must not be that obvious if so many followers are misled. We all want to believe, "It's not me, or it's the other guy in that church that is deceived." So here is the question the Spirit has me to ask people, "Do you believe your pastor teaches 100 percent Gospel truth without any error?" To those who answered no, the Spirit had me to ask, "Do you know what he taught that was wrong?" Of course, the majority answered, "No." So if you do not understand that what is being taught is wrong, you will tell others the same wrong information! Most nondenominational churches believe that the Catholic Church doctrine is the worst in the Christian church, and so do most of the evangelical churches that broke off from the Catholic Church.

Ask yourself, "what church or denomination would Jesus choose as His true church?" Now, you may say the church you are affiliated with, but have you heard about the Church of Philadelphia mentioned in Revelation chapter 3? This is one of the seven churches that Jesus does not have any fault with. Remember, you have to try the spirit by the Spirit. In 2 Corinthians 11:13-15, Paul reveals a mystery that we need to pay attention to. It is clear that Satan and demons are appearing as true believers. Twisting the truth as he did with Eve in the garden, causing the believer to walk in the wrong direction, while believing in his mind he is saved and in good hands! False teachers bring false doctrines; these principles caused people to believe things that to the intellect sounds good, but spiritually are corruptible. Satan reasoned with Eve to convince her to eat of the fruit that was forbidden by God. This is easy for a Christian to see; the Gay Agenda is trying to say that God accepts their lifestyle of homosexuality based on the relationship King David had with Jonathan (King Saul's son) where it mentions that "David loved Jonathan." So they say, "this is proof that these young men were lovers" (1 Sam.18-20). You see how the intellect can comprehend information and be spiritually wrong.

It's easy to see the fault in this interpretation of scripture, but how about some you believed in? The Bible speaks of line upon line, precept upon precept, that is, truth upon truth. If any line is broken by another precept, then that teaching is wrong. (Remember in division, if one step is wrong in your calculation, then the answer will also be wrong.) Paul instructed us to rightly divide the Word; therefore, it can be divided wrongly. One of the biggest doctrines these false teachers are teaching is the doctrine of "Prosperity" or now "The Blessings of God." Every time you turn your radio or television on to a Christian station, someone is speaking about finances. This is not by chance! It is written in scripture, "The time will come when they will teach that prosperity will be the sign that God favors you" (1 Tim. 6:3-10). This type of teaching shapes us into the Church of Laodicea found in Revelation 3:14-22. Christ said to them, "Because you sayest, I am rich, and increased with goods, and have need of nothing." The Spirit asked me a question, "How did the people become this way?" Let us look at this Church, how did they end up believing that because they were "prosperous" or "blessed" that Jesus was a part of them? If you look closely, we see Jesus outside of this church knocking on the doors to come in! The people had no idea this was so! They were feeling as if everything was good as they sang praises and gave offerings, and testified how God blessed them—sounds like most churches today.

Again, how did people accept this teaching? By their teachers or leaders of course! They were deceived by the craftiness of clever manipulation of God's Word. If you are old enough, you may remember a doctrine called "Have a Need, Plant a Seed." Based on the idea that if you wanted an "apple tree," you have to plant apple seeds; or if you want an orange tree, you have to plant orange seeds. So if you want an apple tree, you don't plant orange seeds.

Makes good intellectual sense, right? If you want a car, then give a car; if you want money, then give money. So money is a type of literal seed planted with faith, then you shall receive thirty, sixty, one hundred times back. To our intellectual ears this makes sense (or cents). So who would not want that kind of interest on their money? Apply this precept to the Spirit of Jesus's teachings and this "have a need Gospel" does not add up. The precept of Christ's teachings has no bearing on gaining material bliss. Read Mark chapter 4, the seed represents God's word of salvation and the fruit of the Spirit as found in Galatians chapter 5. Jesus said, "My word is Spirit and Life" not money and wealth. Nowhere in the New Testament does Christ refer to His Word to obtain financial bliss. The teaching "give and it shall be given to you" is not referring to money! It is the good news of God's Kingdom to man. By giving and sharing the Word, you will increase in the knowledge and power of God's will.

Check this precept out with the rest of the teachings of Jesus and the apostles. These false teachers twisted the Word of God to consume it upon their own lust for material wealth. They will have people testify to the audience about how God blessed them when they gave to the ministry, how God blessed them with a new car or house, etc., causing a frenzy among believers, so they can obtain their blessing. Like someone in a casino hitting jackpot, causing everyone who hears the bell to play harder, hoping they will be the next big winner! Well, who ends up with the biggest pot? It's the pastor of course! Can you imagine Jesus riding in a golden chariot instead of a donkey during His triumphant entry? Look how Jesus spoke of John the Baptist, "Who did you go out to see, a man dressed in King's clothing?"

As we know, John dressed with camel hair and ate wild locust and honey! The final wrench in the gears of gaining wealth is the example Jesus gave in Luke 12:15, "*Take heed, and beware of covetousness; for a man's life consisteth not in the abundance of the things which he possesseth.*" Yet these false preachers teach otherwise; you see how the precepts of Christ contradicts the "get wealth" scheme. He says your life is not about what you posses on earth but what you posses in heaven; Jesus say that where a man's heart is, there will his treasures be. Jesus also taught us not to store up treasures here on earth, but store up your treasures in heaven. You can actually build on this precept, and this line will never be broken; try it, I'm confident in the Holy Spirit of what I write to you.

Satan is clever, **he wants you to believe you can serve two masters, money and God**. So does God want us poor? Let the Word of God answer that question. Jesus says, "For God knows what things you have need of before you ask; and seek you first the kingdom of God, and all the things you have need of will be given you." God will meet your need, not your greed! There are men saying that the Bible speaks of money more than any other subject! Maybe that's why so many ministers speak on the subject. If it is true, it is definitely not the most important. If you can see through these false teachers' lies, the message to God's children is not that they all can be millionaires here on earth because everyone would want to be one, a

Christian that is! That's why Jesus said, "Hardly will a rich man enter into the kingdom of God." The truth is, "have a need," and God will meet it! Jesus even said, "If we being evil know how to give good gifts to our children, how much more will My Father give to them that ask Him." Again, can you see how the line was broken about "have a need, plant a seed" by the principles of the Word? Remember it is our responsibility to try the doctrine we believe in with the Holy Spirit as our guide.

A big problem I've noticed is, when a person receives a revelation from the Spirit, they usually go to a source of their affiliation to ask about it. That is like a chicken going to the foxes to complain about their rights! They will only reason with you about it and most likely convince you that what you received is in error. This is a terrible matrix! How can anyone escape their religious institution without rejection from close friends? Jesus says you must be able to forsake anyone for the Kingdom of Heaven's sake. Trust God to lead you into all truth as He said He would. If you ask for an egg, God will not give you a serpent! These teachings of "prosperity" are one of the biggest problems in the body of Christ, and I will discuss the next one in detail in the next chapter.

# Chapter 4

## SATAN'S TRICK EXPOSED

In the book of Acts chapter 15 (please read), we can see a prophecy of what Jesus was referring to in the parable of the "good seed." In Matthew 13:25-30, He says that a wicked servant planted tares among the wheat. The "tares" represent the "lies" and the "wheat" represents "truth," so Jesus says to let them both grow together. This parable also represents "the harvest," in which you can see "good Christians" and "bad ones"; the bad ones represent Christians who were deceived by Satan. Connect this to Mark 4 and Matthew 24. When Christ was referring to those being deceived, He was not just speaking of the lost in this world, but those who believed in Him.

Now let's look at Satan's trick in Acts 15. You will see there was a problem about the Gentiles' (non-Jewish people) conversion in Christ. Some Jews were saying that the Gentiles had to be circumcised and follow the "Whole Law of Moses" that is the "Old Covenant." But as we can see, this was not God's plan. Even Peter had a vision of God saving the Gentiles as in Acts chapter 10 and 11. He was sent to Cornelius's house to witness to that household. Then Peter had to give an explanation to Jewish leaders on why he had been in the Gentiles' home; because it was against Jewish law to enter into the gentiles home, for they were considered unclean. Satan's trick was to mix the "Old Testament" works with the "New Testament" of Jesus's teachings, which is faith in Him alone for "salvation." Now this clever trick has reached us here today!

The majority of our churches are practicing these things and teaching them to you. Read Matthew 9:16-17; again here is another "prophetic burp." Jesus was warning us what will happen in the future after He had died! Hopefully, it is easy for you to see that Jesus is referring to the "Old Covenant" or Testament and the New Covenant. Paul had to rebuke Peter for not standing up to the truth when faced with the Pharisees on the issues. Read James 2:10-13, the scriptures plainly state that if you break the law in one point, you are guilty of breaking the whole law. Also, if you keep the law at one point, you have to obey the whole law! Then if you put yourself under the law, you are not under grace! Paul addressed this to the Jews in Rome. So Paul and other apostles revealed Satan's plan back then, but if you know our enemy, he did not give up, he just changed strategies.

I see so many denominations keeping and teaching Old Covenant laws to their flock; some are worse than others such as the dietary laws in Leviticus, the Sabbath day and weeks, to how woman should dress, mixing races of people; the list could go on for pages. There is one law almost every church practices about 99 percent, even cults practice this law. Remember Satan's strategy has changed, but Satan has not changed! If you operate under the law, you are not under grace; so to make it plain, his plan is to have the believer practice the law and have him believe he is under grace at the same time! So what law from the Old Testament does Satan have everyone practicing? Now what I'm about to share, you may have to research on your own, but I believe it is the cleverest one Satan uses because many will stumble at it. Let us start from the scripture almost every church uses, Malachi 3:8-11 (surprised?) "Will a man rob God? Yet you have robbed Me. But ye say, 'Wherein have we robbed Thee?'" 'In Tithes and offerings.'" **"You are cursed with a curse**: for you have robbed Me, even this whole nation." Now the question I pose to you is, "How are you cursed?"

As we have read, the Jewish people were under the Law of Moses and commanded to follow the whole law to receive the "blessings of Abraham" under the covenant which was made. Now let's look at what we have been taught today. I'm positive all who are in church heard this scripture from Malachi being read and made a point in giving unto the Lord. A majority of preachers testify that the reason everything is going wrong in your life is because you have not paid your tithes. (Let me make this clear; there is nothing wrong with giving God a tenth of your income or for that matter 1 to 100 percent of your

income. If that is what the Spirit is laying upon your heart
to give.) You will have to give an account of earnings in
the day of judgment, not for salvation but for rewards of
faithfulness, and there is nothing wrong in being faithful
in giving a tithe unto the Lord. As Paul said in Romans,
"The law is good," but to tithe under the law is dangerous
for you, for then must you follow the whole law, and then
you are not under grace but the law! Because the only
way you can be **"cursed with a curse"** is be under the Law!
In Galatians 3:13, Paul makes it plain to us, **"Christ has
redeemed us from the curse of the law**, being made a curse
for us: for it is written, 'Cursed is every one that hangeth
on a tree.'" Line upon line, precept upon precept, so the
preachers try to put fear in you to get your hard-earned
money so they can build "mega churches" and live like
kings and queens.

They teach tithing as if this is the only unforgivable sin
and that by not tithing according to Malachi, this curse
supersedes the work of Christ on the cross! Paul asked
the Galatians, **"Who has bewitched you! Did you receive
the Spirit by the works of the law, or by the hearing of
faith?** Are you so foolish? Having begun in the Spirit,
are you now made perfect under the flesh?" (The flesh
is in reference to your obedience to the law.) Of course,
the answer is by faith, or this should be the answer. This
should give you new insight to the things written in the
Epistles. Do you understand what I am trying to say? **"You
receive the blessings of Abraham by faith in Christ alone
not by observing the law!"** Just as your salvation is based
on faith in Jesus's redemptive work. Satan is trying to get

you to work for what you receive freely from God! All the Epistles agree! You see, Satan changed the strategy from obeying the "whole law" to obeying "part of the law" because as the Spirit revealed if you follow any part of the law, you are obligated to follow the whole law. Look at what Paul says in Gal. 3:10-12. People had a hard time understanding the true work of Christ; the Jews in Rome thought Paul was saying it was okay to sin, that grace may abound. Remember you have the right to give unto the Lord ten percent, just do it out of love and not because of fear of being cursed. Because if you receive these precepts, you are free. As it is said, "Where the Spirit of the Lord is, there is Liberty!"

I have met preachers who preached tithing for ten years straight or made the issue of money a weekly conversation. One in particular went from two thousand members to five hundred because as one of the deacons told me, "We just got tired of hearing about finances all the time." I can imagine, every time you go to church or turn on your radio or TV, that is the main message you see or hear. False teachers even try to use the teachings of Jesus to justify why you have to tithe! So if you are not blessed, it must be something you are doing wrong! Did you know according to the law of tithing, you were to bring it to a place God has appointed and EAT IT! That's right. Consume it upon your lust, read it for yourself in Deuteronomy 14:22-26; bet you didn't receive this instruction from your minister! So what happens if a Jewish person in the Old Testament tithed and committed adultery? Would they receive the blessing of God? According to the Epistle of James, if you offend the law in one point, you are a transgressor of the whole law. Therefore, the blessing of Abraham is cancelled for that Jewish person. Even today, would you reward your child cake and ice cream if he or she stole money out of your wallet? Even if they completed all their chores?

The law was given to the natural seed of Abraham by Moses, and under this covenant, they were obligated to keep the whole law in the first five books of Moses. We, who are non-Jewish, were not of this covenant. So the final way to get you under part of the law is to prove Jesus ordained tithing. In Luke 11:41-42, these clever preachers twist what Jesus said to the Pharisees. In fact, Jesus was rebuking them for the way they practiced the teachings of "law." Our leaders today say that in verse 42, "these ought you to have done, and not leave the others undone," that this scripture is referring to the fact that Jesus was ordaining tithing! How were we so naïve? Jesus was referring to how God wanted them to walk while under the Covenant of Moses and how badly the leaders missed the mark. Jesus was referring to how the Pharisees performed God's duties! Not ordaining tithing to the New Covenant saints. Remember, these men of today "Cut and Paste Scripture" out of context to prove a point. Nowhere in the Epistles do the apostles teach this to the Gentiles other than the Jews who were wrongly teaching the Gentiles to come under the law and pay tithes. As pointed out before, I pray that as you continue to study this you will receive freedom.

# Chapter 5

## THE CHURCH AND MONEY

The scriptures mentioned a few things concerning giving for the necessity of the needy, but never did the apostles take money from the offering to live lavishly off the people's giving. In order to get the most money out of you, they find it easy to put a yoke of the law on you and twist the idea of giving, so you can gain all the material wealth you can; then the more you gain the more you will tithe. In other words as you increase, so do they. There is a major problem when so much teaching and preaching about finances is spreading throughout the body of Christ. Remember, this will produce a specific character in the believer that will cause them to stumble in their faith. Now we have heard that the love of money is the root of all evil. Another translation may say all kinds of evil. With this in mind, let's think about what Jesus mentioned in Mark chapter 4 in the parable of "The Sower." As said before, the seed represents the Word. Jesus uses simple things to confound the wise or confuse them.

If you know anything about planting seeds, then you know that seeds produce roots for the gathering of moisture for the plant to grow. So if the love of money is the root of all kinds of evil, imagine the **SEED!** To give you a hint, go all the way back to the Garden of Eden when God was questioning Adam and Eve about their sin. Remember, God asked Adam, "What did YOU do?" Adam replied, "The woman YOU gave me, handed me the fruit and I ate of it" (of course I'm paraphrasing here). Then God asked Eve, "What is it you have done?" She replied, "The serpent, he tricked me, and I did eat." Did you see it? What the seed really is! If you guessed, it's **SELFISHNESS!** The preachers are making the saints appear selfish. Let's take a look at one of the scriptures they use. "Give and it shall be given unto you." This verse is used by them to refer to money. Now hear with your spirit, "Give money and money will be given to you" sounds okay to the intellectual ears. But again, this is spiritually wrong. Look at Luke 6:37-42 and Matthew 7:1-20. You will see that the context of Jesus's speech is not about money but about faith and judgment. Think what Jesus said when He spoke, "Build your treasures in Heaven, not on earth." Does this agree with "give money and you shall receive money here on earth"? Again, think about your motive for giving; why are you giving? Is it to gain something in return? Again, I say deception is not that obvious. Jesus is not contradicting Himself, false teachers are interpreting the scriptures incorrectly, and as you have learned, the line is broken by the Spirit of Truth.

In fact, if you look closely at what Jesus said, all you have to do is ask and believe God will give it, and you shall have it. Jesus never asked amiss as James mentioned in the first chapter. He always consulted with His Father about what He wanted, and this is our example for following how to pray. Instead, we ask like children who want everything they see. Now let us look at a teaching these false teachers preach called **The Hundredfold Return.** Again, we look at Mark chapter 4 (this is the parable that Jesus said, "if you did not understand; how can you interpret any other parable") where Jesus said the seed that fell on good ground brought forth thirty-, sixty-, and a hundredfold. Notice the text of what Jesus is talking about. As you can see, He is not talking about money or finances but about the fruit of the Spirit as found in Galatians chapter 5. So these false preachers twist what Christ taught in order to feed upon your desire to gain wealth. Almost everyone wants to be financially wealthy, and they use this basic desire with the incorrect meaning from scripture to give you the hope of being "blessed." When someone drives a nice BMW and they are saved, most people would say, "God has truly blessed you, Brother," and the response is "Amen." Unconsciously, this situation is saying that because of a material possession, this is equated to being favored by God! In 1 Timothy 6:1-10, you cannot come to the conclusion of this one hundredfold return.

The Kingdom of God is righteousness, peace and joy in the Holy Ghost; where is money in this equation? The prophecy in Timothy is at hand! This teaching is leading us right into the attitudes of the Laodiceans who felt that because they were blessed, God was with them, but **Jesus was outside** knocking to come into that church! Like I mentioned previously, selfishness is the end result, so the church that ended up "blessed" with material wealth was "EMPTY" of Christ! Take a look at today's church record: 75 percent divorce rate (This includes pastors and some of them marry a member of their church after divorcing their previous spouse!), singles ministries have to shut down because they were havens for all kinds of sexual sins among the single members, choir members fighting and backbiting, pastors busted for molesting men and young girls, and deacons firing their pastors for teaching what they feel is inappropriate.

I could write a book about sins that are in the church, but as you can see, the root of the problem is, there is not enough substance from the pulpit to help the followers overcome their selfish desires. Ministers are too busy building million dollar complex centers to hold concerts and private schools for the purpose of gaining business or do I dare to say earning revenue. What has happened to the type of ministry Christ laid down for us to follow? If you remember, when Jesus read from the scripture, "I have come to feed the poor, open the eyes of the blind, to heal the sick, etc." The apostles followed what Christ laid down, but from there to here, we messed things up just like the Jews of Moses's time till Christ. The religious leaders messed things up, and Jesus rebuked them for it. How is it now almost every minister wants a megachurch, radio and TV ministry, and a world outreach ministry? Have they become fascinated with their name or something?

Coming up in minister training, the idea of running the church like a business came up in the early nineties. A business is about what? Making money of course. The love of money is also causing this prophecy to fulfill itself; "The love of many will grow cold" (Matt. 24:11-12). One of the greatest things Jesus said to help us in these times is found in Luke 16:13-15, which states, "You cannot serve God and money, either you will love one and hate the other, you cannot serve two masters." I used to always wonder why Jesus said that and not, "you cannot serve two gods like God and Buddha" or something of that sort. The revelation that the love of money is a type of "idolatry" that stretches all the way to the "whore of Babylon" is the reason Jesus warned us not to store up treasures here on earth but in heaven.

Can't you see? Jesus is trying to protect us from what He knew would come upon the earth! The church is already inside the "whore of Babylon"! These false teachers have set us up for the future fulfillment of Revelation 18:1-19. With their "blessing scheme," we end up hearing a voice from heaven warning us to "come out of her, my people, that you be not partakers of her sins." The question you have to ask yourself is, "How come no one from the churches knew they were in the whore?" Where are the leaders of the churches and better yet where are you? The answer is, they are deceived and deceiving many as Jesus has said, "False teachers and preachers shall deceive many." Remember, it is your responsibility to protect yourself from this untoward generation.

Ever noticed how people who are wealthy in your church are admonished? I visited a church where a pastor did such a thing; the person he admonished used direct deposit to give to the offering. I noticed after the service, this person was upset because the pastor exposed their business without their permission and rightfully so. It is not hidden what this pastor was trying to advocate to the rest of the church members to follow that example. Because we are headed to a cashless society, churches have ATM machines put inside so no excuses can be used not to give in the offering. Some churches have two or more offerings a service. I have visited a few where the deacon would say, "We did not meet our quota for this offering." And he was asking people if they could give $100 all the way down to $5! I have seen greater atrocities than these! He that has an ear, let him hear what the Spirit is saying to the churches.

Open your eyes, the church is already in the whore. They are having sexual idolatry with her (an intimate relationship with money). Praise be to God that He has graciously warned us and protected us with His Word from the dangers of this dangerous time. We have to use God's Word to keep ourselves without spot or wrinkle.

# A Word to the Church
## From the book of Jeremiah

An appalling, wonderful, and horrible thing has happened! The preachers preach falsely and pastors act as lord over My flock, and My people love it this way, but what will your end be?

Behold, you are trusting in deceitful words, for my people are foolish and have no understanding. They are stupid children and shrewd to do evil, but to follow My Spirit they do not know.

Wicked rulers are found among My people; they build churches, they set a trap, they catch men and women like a cage full of birds. Their teachings are full of poison, and these ministers have become great! And rich!

All of them are greedy for gain; everyone from the fivefold ministry, even to the helps, everyone practices deceit. They preach that wealth is the sign that God has blessed you, they turn the "living waters" into molten silver and gold. The blood of Christ to the way of riches, and because of needs, My people follow this abomination.

Did I not say, "Labor not for meat that will perish, but for meat that leads to everlasting life; You cannot serve two masters; either you will serve one and hate the other; You cannot serve money and Me."

I know what things you have need of before you ask, for if I take care of birds that do not plant seeds or work the fields, but yet they are provided for. I know how to take care of what belongs to Me! You are worth more than many birds, My children.

Seek me more than riches, and you shall prosper in the Spirit, for I AM a Spirit and I desire for you to worship Me in spirit and in truth. Then shall you be a true worshipper, then shall you be rich with faith. You shall be My king and priest, for I made you a new Spirit; My Hands formed you. Those of you who have an ear, hear what the Spirit is saying. The children of Israel desired a king to rule over them, just as My children do today. This is why I gave you My Spirit, to lead and guide you; therefore, walk in the Spirit and you will be free from the cage and see the traps to avoid them; for where My Spirit is, there is liberty!

# Chapter 6

## PROTECTING YOURSELF FROM ERROR

When we read the Bible, it is impossible for your brain (intellect) to comprehend what the Spirit is saying. Paul was telling the intellectuals in Rome in the book of Romans 8:5-14, "For to be carnally minded is death; but to be spiritually minded is life and peace. Because the carnal mind (brain or intellect) is enmity against God, for it is not subject to the law of God, neither indeed can it be." If you can grasp this in the Spirit, you can be delivered from depression or any form of hardship that the mind imagines. The brain only thinks of what it wants, from the experiences of your five senses, it cares nothing about your eternal salvation. Since the things that are spiritual cannot feed the brain anything from the five senses, there is nothing the brain can desire spiritually.

Try reading the Bible for hours and see what happens, especially at night. Then put in a video you have been wanting to watch, and see what happens. Which one will put you to sleep the quickest? The brain will feed off entertainment before something spiritual. Your spirit actually has a lot more power than your flesh! As it is written, "Greater is He in you, than he that is of the world." When you read the words of Jesus, how does your mind perceive it? Do you really see who is talking with you when you see the red letters (if your bible prints the words of Jesus in red)? You are reading the WORDS OF GOD HIMSELF! The Great Creator, speaking to man! He is giving us instructions and warnings to protect ourselves from these dangerous times. Just like a natural father would do for his own son, in whom he loves. So when you read the Word, try to let the Spirit whom God gave you to open your mind to the fullness of what God has to share.

In Matthew chapter 24, we see the deceptive power of darkness fooling the world's nations and especially the church. God had to shorten the length of days of the great deceiver, or the very elect of God would be deceived. Seeing how convincing Satan will be, to whom do you put your trust in—your pastor, bishop, or prophet? It would be wise to listen to the voice of Jesus. As He said, "They that hear My voice are my sheep." Allow the Holy Spirit to lead and guide you through the valley of the shadow of death.

Remember what I said earlier, God's word is for our protection. Here are two commandments that will protect you: Love God with all your heart, mind, soul, and strength; and love your neighbor as yourself. Allow the Spirit to produce fruit in your life. All the Christian values are hinged on these three ways of life. Like Paul wrote, "What good is it, if you give all your money to the poor (or ministry) and have not the Love of God in your life or love your neighbor as yourself." What value does casting out devils or healing the sick, if you do not love God with all your heart, mind, and soul? These are they that will hear what Jesus says to them in the day of judgement, "Depart from Me, you workers of iniquity, I do not know you."

How valuable is your soul worth to you? How much effort do you put into a message heard from the pulpit? As you can see, it is going to take some effort from you not to be deceived. By meditating on the things of God, studying, praising, and giving Him thanks will help you from stumbling and being tossed to and fro with every wind of doctrine out there.

Take a look at attitudes concerning the Word of God: children can spend three hours on video games, woman can shop for hours, men can spend hours watching sports, yet in church, no one can stand being there for more than an hour! As we can figure out, where is the love of God in this? As I have mentioned before, no one can serve two masters; you can't love God and money, or sex, entertainment, and material things. God gave His Word as a measuring rod to show you whether you really love Him or not. God bases your love for Him out of obedience and commitment to His Word. If you are a victim of the "prosperity message," Jesus offers a word that will help you.

Christ says in Luke 12:15, "Take heed [pay attention; set your heart to understand] and beware of covetousness, for a man's life consisteth not in the abundance of the things he possesseth." This word from Jesus is the wrench in the "blessing business" and the short circuit in the "finance scheme"; also look at verses 22 to 23 and 29 to 34, it says, "For where your treasure is, there will your heart be also." Also you may recall the scripture that says, "Out of the abundance of a man's heart, his mouth will speak."

So if all you hear about is some form of money coming from your church leaders, you can know what is the main objective of the leader's heart. Again, if you are one who was seeking wealth, believing this was God's plan, just ask for forgiveness and ask God to create in you a clean heart. Train yourself to set your affections on the things of God, not on the things of this life. Pray that the Holy Spirit will lead and guide you through these dark times.

## The Two Greatest Commandments

The amazing thing that happened before writing this book and during the concept of this word, I had asked Christians what are the two greatest commandments. Would you believe that over 95 percent of them did not know! Even some pastors and deacons! This was not asked to brag or belittle someone, but to show how the most important matters of God's Word are not in the forefront of our mind or in the church today. How can you practice a way of life if it is not common knowledge? The sad truth is, you can't. The greatest two commandments are the following: "To love God with all your heart, mind, soul, and strength" and "Love your neighbor as yourself." If you have been truly born again by the power of God, this would not be a commandment but a way of life.

When you lose your way, then it is a commandment to lead you back to the life in Christ. This is one of the three keys to sustain you in these dangerous times. Notice in the commandment, it does not say, "Love your pastor, bishop, or whoever your leader is, with all your heart, mind and soul." But people do this without noticing they are doing this very act. Most churchgoers say, "My pastor or my bishop says . . ." Hardly do I hear people say, "The Holy Spirit shared this with me from the Bible." It seems as though people have replaced their "leaders" in place of the Spirit. Don't misunderstand what I am saying here. God has given us leaders, but leaders are exercising authority over us and this is what Jesus taught His apostles not to do. Even Peter wrote, "Do not act as Lord over the flock." I have seen a lot of women who have placed their pastor over their husband. Some of these pastors know this and will not correct this error! All kinds of errors are in the church as a direct result of disobeying the greatest commandments.

So how do we love God with all our heart (spirit)? with all our mind? with all our soul? First, you have to tear down your way of thinking or the way you were taught to think. Then, renew your mind with the mind of Christ. Read 1 Corinthians 2:16, notice that Paul says we have the mind of Christ! Yet Paul instructed in another passage of scripture to "let this mind be in you that was in Christ Jesus." It was evident that the majority of believers did not understand this, even today, this is true for us. Where does Christ dwell in you? Did you say or think, "In my spirit"? So if Christ dwells in your spirit, and your spirit has access to your mind, then guess what? Jesus has access to your mind! Glory be to God, this is one of the "great mysteries" of the Old Testament. This is what the scriptures mean where it is written, "Greater is He that is in you, than he that is in the world." This is why you have all the power of the kingdom of God dwelling in you because Jesus is in your spirit! When you read the Bible, allow the Spirit that was in Christ to reveal to you how you are walking in the Spirit.

When you see something that personally applies to you when reading the scriptures, repent and keep moving on until you have read the New Testament at least three times. The truth shall set you free, and as long as you walk in the Spirit, you will never fall or stumble. Think about it; will the Holy Spirit lead you to believe a lie? Of course not, the Holy Spirit will empower you to control your soul (the realm of the mind) to the obedience of God's will just as Jesus said, "I do what my Father shows me." Now how did His Father show Him His will? By Jesus spending time with Him in prayer, meditating, professing as in Psalm 119; by the way, Jesus read the Psalms and Proverbs, which you should make these very books fit into your life. Another way to help yourself is to hear the word; listen to the Bible on CD or cassette or MP3 and take notes, especially what the Spirit reveals to you about yourself.

The second commandment is to love your neighbor as you love yourself. If we all did this, there would be no division in the body of Christ! Just ask yourself, would you want anyone to steal from you? Would you want anyone to harm your family? How about someone cheating you out of your money? Of course not, but this is why the world is so crazy.

People are doing things to others they do not want done to them. In the Epistle of John, he makes a statement, "How can a man say, he loves God whom he cannot see and hate his neighbor whom he can see." John goes on to say, "This man is a liar and the truth is not in him." Yet some people who call themselves Christians hate other races! It should be obvious as to why these two commandments are the greatest two. God is Love; and if you say, you love Him, then you would love your neighbor. If the love you have for God was always on your mind, how could you lust, steal, commit fornication or any other sin? If everyone would do unto others as they would have others do to them, the whole earth would be at peace. What man would cheat on his wife? If he did not want his wife to cheat on him. What man would molest an innocent child? If he did not want his child molested. Everything that Jesus said about the "last days" are a direct breakdown of these two commandments.

My intentions in this book are to help you see some not-so-obvious teachings, not to keep you from fellowshipping with others, and to help you understand the importance of studying everything you hear from the pulpit. God bless you as you search for the truth.

# Prophecy's Concerning Jesus

| | |
|---|---|
| Gen. 3:14-15; 21 | Ps. 8:1-6 |
| Gen. 22:1-14 | Ps. 18:2,50 |
| Gen. 37:28-29 | Ps. 22:1-19 |
| Exod. 12:13 | Ps. 24:1-6 |
| Exod. 16:4; 17:6 | Ps. 25:8-9 |
| Lev. 9:9; 16:30 | Ps. 30:3 |
| Num. 21:8-9 | Ps. 31:18 |
| Deut. 32:3-4 | Ps. 132:11 |
| Ps. 2:6-7 | Isa. 9:6-7 |
| Ps. 3:1-2 | Isa. 7:14 |
| Ps. 6:4-5 | Isa. 53:3 |
| Isa. 61:1-2 | Isa. 53:1 |
| Hos. 11:1 | Zech. 9:9 |

There are many more prophecies concerning Jesus as the Messiah; this is what Paul was telling Timothy to study that he may prove with all the scriptures that Jesus is Lord and our deliverer. The prophecies of Christ will strengthen your personal faith and walk, so find others and find where they were fulfilled by Jesus. Be sure to look for my next book, *What God Created, When He Created You.*

To arrange speaking engagements for
Tyrone Everett at your church or fellowship
contact 904-282-8510 or email
TYNCHRIST4U@YAHOO.COM